Title Page

Title: The Politics of Power: Recognizing Greed and Choosing Ethical Leaders
Author: Rializa Fabiania-Sabido
Publisher: RB Publishing
Location: Isulan, Sultan Kudarat, Philippines
Date: August, 2024

Copyright Page

The Politics of Power: Recognizing Greed and Choosing Ethical Leaders
© 2024 by Rializa Fabiania-Sabido
All rights reserved.

No part of this publication may be reproduced, distributed, or transmitted in any form or by any means, including photocopying, recording, or other electronic or mechanical methods, without the prior written permission of the publisher, except in the case of brief quotations embodied in critical reviews and certain other non-commercial uses permitted by copyright law. For permission requests, write to the publisher at the email address below:

RB Publishing
rializa953@gmail.com

First Edition: August, 2024
ISBN: 9798336148480

Disclaimer:

The content of this book is intended for informational and educational purposes only. The views and opinions expressed in this book are those of the author and are based on personal research and experience. They do not necessarily reflect the official policy or position of any organization, group, or individual mentioned within. The examples, case studies, and references are used to illustrate points and should not be interpreted as endorsements or criticisms of any particular person or entity.

The author and publisher make no representations or warranties with respect to the accuracy, applicability, fitness, or completeness of the contents of this book. The reader is encouraged to verify the information independently and seek professional advice where appropriate. The author and publisher shall not be liable for any damages or losses arising from the use of this book or its contents.

All rights to the content, design, and intellectual property of this book are reserved by the author and publisher. Unauthorized use or reproduction of any part of this book without permission is strictly prohibited.

Acknowledgments

The creation of this book has been a journey of learning, reflection, and dedication, and it would not have been possible without the unwavering support and encouragement of some truly special people in my life.

First and foremost, I want to express my deepest gratitude to my husband, Ruel Sabido. Your steadfast support, love, and belief in me have been my guiding light throughout this entire process. Thank you for standing by my side, for your endless patience, and for inspiring me to persevere even when the road was challenging. I am so grateful to share this journey with you.

To my family, your constant encouragement and understanding have been a source of strength for me. Thank you for giving me the space and support to pursue this dream.

I also want to extend my heartfelt thanks to my dear friends, Rev. Ptr. Joel P. Bernardo and Carmelito Santiago. Your faith in me, your wishes, and your prayers have lifted my spirits and kept me going. Rev. Ptr. Joel, your belief in my ability to bring this book to life has been a powerful motivator, and Carmelito, your friendship and support have meant the world to me.

This book is as much yours as it is mine, and I am forever grateful for your love, prayers, and encouragement.

Table of Contents

1. **Introduction: Why Leadership Matters More Than Ever**
   - The Reality We Face: Understanding Today's Leadership Crisis
   - The Purpose of This Book: Equipping Citizens for Informed Choices
2. **Chapter 1: Power in the Real World – What It Is and How It Affects Us**
   - The True Nature of Power: Influence Beyond Authority
   - Everyday Power Dynamics: How Leadership Shapes Communities
   - The Consequences of Power: Decisions That Change Lives
3. **Chapter 2: The Greed Trap – When Leaders Lose Their Way**
   - Greed in Action: Recognizing the Shift from Service to Selfishness
   - Case Studies of Corruption: Real-World Examples of Greedy Leadership
   - The Impact on Us: How Greedy Leaders Hurt Communities
4. **Chapter 3: Real Traits of Ethical Leaders – What We Should Look For**
   - Integrity in Action: The Hallmarks of Honest Leadership
   - Transparency and Trust: Why Open Leaders Build Stronger Societies
   - Making a Difference: How Ethical Leaders Impact Real Lives
5. **Chapter 4: Seeing Through the Lies – Identifying Greedy Leaders**
   - Spotting Red Flags: The Warning Signs of Self-Interest in Leadership
   - Real-World Comparisons: Examples of Ethical vs. Greedy Leadership
   - Tools for Today: Practical Ways to Evaluate Leaders in Your Community
6. **Chapter 5: Our Role in Shaping Leadership – The Power of Community Action**
   - Creating a Culture of Accountability: How Communities Can Demand Better
   - The Strength of Civic Engagement: Real Stories of Change from the Ground Up
   - Keeping Leaders in Check: Effective Strategies for Ensuring Responsibility
7. **Chapter 6: The Real-World Impact of Leadership Choices**
   - Stories of Success and Failure in Leadership
   - The Long-Term Effects of Ethical vs. Unethical Leadership
   - Unethical Leadership and its Devastating Consequences
8. **Chapter 7: How to Choose Leaders Who Won't Let Us Down**
   - Doing Your Homework: How to Research and Understand Candidates
   - Making Your Voice Count: The Reality of Voting and Participation
   - Building a Movement: Organizing Communities for Ethical Leadership
9. **Chapter 8: The Changing Landscape – What's Next for Leadership?**
   - Adapting to Change: How Modern Challenges Are Redefining Leadership
   - Technology's Role: The Reality of Social Media and Misinformation
   - Vigilance is Key: Staying Involved in an Ever-Changing World

10. **Chapter 9: Conclusion – Taking Control of Our Future**
    - Reflecting on Reality: What We've Learned About Leadership
    - The Citizen's Responsibility: How We Can All Make a Difference
    - Preparing for Tomorrow: The Future We Can Build Together
    - Final Call to Action: Empowering You to Demand Ethical Leadership
    - Closing Thoughts: Why Your Role in Leadership Matters
11. **Final Note**
12. **Appendices**
13. **Index**
14. **About the Author**

Introduction: Why Leadership Matters More Than Ever

The Reality We Face: Understanding Today's Leadership Crisis

In today's world, the challenges we face are more complex and interconnected than ever before. Political polarization, economic inequality, and social unrest have created an environment where the quality of leadership can determine the success or failure of entire communities. Leaders wield significant power, and the way they choose to use that power has a profound impact on the lives of millions.

However, not all leaders are driven by a desire to serve the public good. Many are motivated by greed, using their positions to further their own interests at the expense of those they are supposed to lead. This crisis of leadership calls for a renewed focus on ethical governance, where integrity, transparency, and accountability are paramount.

The Purpose of This Book: Equipping Citizens for Informed Choices

This book aims to empower you, the reader, to recognize the signs of ethical and unethical leadership. By understanding the dynamics of power and the traits that define ethical leaders, you will be better equipped to make informed decisions in the voting booth and in your community. This book is not just for political enthusiasts or those with a background in government; it is for anyone who cares about the future of their community and wants to play an active role in shaping it.

Through real-world examples, practical advice, and actionable steps, this book will guide you in identifying leaders who prioritize the common good over personal gain. Whether you're evaluating local officials, state representatives, or national leaders, the principles outlined in this book will help you discern who truly deserves your support.

Chapter 1: Power in the Real World – What It Is and How It Affects Us

The True Nature of Power: Influence Beyond Authority

Power is a concept that often evokes images of authority, control, and dominance. It's easy to think of power as something reserved for world leaders, corporate executives, or high-ranking officials. However, the true nature of power extends far beyond these traditional roles. At its core, power is the ability to influence outcomes, shape decisions, and drive change—whether on a global stage or within a small community.

Power manifests in various forms, from the visible acts of governance—such as passing laws or setting policies—to the subtle ways in which people and institutions influence behavior and shape cultural norms. This influence can be wielded for the benefit of the greater good or for personal gain, depending on the motivations and ethical compass of those who hold it.

Understanding power as a tool of influence rather than just a position of authority is crucial. This broader perspective allows us to recognize that power can be exercised by anyone, in any context. A community leader organizing a local food drive, a teacher inspiring students to reach their potential, or a social media influencer raising awareness for a cause—all are examples of individuals wielding power to effect change.

The implications of this understanding are significant. If power is about influence, then everyone who can affect the thoughts, behaviors, or actions of others holds a certain degree of power. This realization broadens the scope of who we consider powerful and emphasizes the importance of ethical behavior in even the smallest acts of leadership.

Everyday Power Dynamics: How Leadership Shapes Communities

Power dynamics are at play in every community, from small towns to bustling cities. While we often associate power with national or global leaders, it is just as critical—and perhaps more immediately impactful—at the local level. Local leaders, such as mayors, council members, and community organizers, wield significant influence over the day-to-day lives of citizens.

These leaders make decisions that affect how public funds are spent, what projects are prioritized, and how resources are distributed. For example, a city council might decide whether to allocate budget funds toward improving public transportation or enhancing local parks. A school board might choose to invest in advanced learning programs or focus on basic infrastructure improvements. Each of these decisions shapes the community in meaningful ways, affecting everything from economic development to social equity.

The impact of leadership is also seen in the informal power structures that exist within communities. Influential community members—such as business owners, religious leaders, or activists—often wield considerable power through their ability to mobilize people, shape public opinion, and advocate for change. These individuals can act as catalysts for positive development or, if driven by self-interest, can exacerbate divisions and tensions within the community.

A clear example of everyday power dynamics can be seen in how local leaders respond to crises. In the wake of a natural disaster, for instance, the effectiveness of a community's recovery efforts often hinges on the decisions made by local leaders. Their ability to coordinate resources, communicate with the public, and prioritize needs can mean the difference between a swift recovery and prolonged suffering. This underscores the importance of having leaders who are not only competent but also committed to serving the public good.

Understanding these dynamics is essential for recognizing the power we all have to influence our communities. Whether through voting, volunteering, or simply participating in local events, each of us has the ability to shape the direction of our community. Recognizing this power empowers us to demand more from our leaders and hold them accountable for their actions.

The Consequences of Power: Decisions That Change Lives

Every exercise of power comes with consequences, both intended and unintended. The decisions made by those in positions of power can change lives in profound ways, influencing everything from individual opportunities to the overall well-being of a community or nation.

Consider, for example, a local government's decision to allocate funds to public transportation versus road infrastructure. Investing in public transportation might make it easier for lower-income residents to commute to work, access healthcare, and participate in community life. On the other hand, prioritizing road infrastructure might benefit those who already own vehicles and can afford to live in areas with better amenities. Both decisions reflect different uses of power, and both have different consequences for the community.

The effects of power are not always immediate. Sometimes, the full impact of a decision is only felt years later. For instance, policies that limit environmental protections may lead to economic growth in the short term but cause long-term damage to public health and the environment. Conversely, decisions that prioritize sustainable practices might require upfront costs but lead to a healthier and more resilient community in the future.

A striking example of the long-term consequences of leadership can be found in educational policy. A leader who prioritizes funding for public schools and access to education for all children is likely to create a more equitable society. Education opens doors to opportunities, reduces poverty, and fosters social mobility. On the other hand, a leader who allows educational resources to be concentrated in wealthier areas may perpetuate cycles of poverty and inequality, limiting opportunities for future generations.

Moreover, the exercise of power can either build trust in institutions or erode it. Leaders who act transparently, communicate openly, and make decisions in the public interest build trust with their constituents. This trust is crucial for the effective functioning of government and society. When people trust their leaders, they are more likely to support policies, comply with regulations, and participate in civic life.

In contrast, when leaders use their power for personal gain, make decisions behind closed doors, or prioritize the interests of a select few, they erode public trust. This erosion can lead to disengagement, cynicism, and even social unrest. The consequences of such leadership can be seen in the rise of populist movements, the decline in voter turnout, and the increasing polarization of societies around the world.

Ultimately, the way power is exercised has profound implications for the fabric of society. Ethical leadership—leadership that prioritizes the common good, acts with transparency, and considers the long-term consequences of decisions—is essential for building strong, vibrant communities. By understanding the nature of power and its impact, we can better evaluate our leaders and hold them accountable for their actions.

Conclusion

Power is a complex and multifaceted force that shapes our world in countless ways. It extends beyond formal authority and is exercised through the everyday decisions that leaders make. Whether at the local or national level, the use of power has profound consequences for individuals, communities, and societies as a whole.

Understanding the nature of power and its impact is the first step in recognizing the importance of ethical leadership. As we continue to explore the dynamics of power in this book, we will delve into how power can be both a force for good and a tool for exploitation, depending on how it is wielded. Recognizing the role of power in our lives equips us to better evaluate our leaders and to demand that they use their power responsibly.

In the next chapter, we will examine how greed can corrupt leaders and lead them to misuse their power, often with devastating consequences for the communities they are supposed to serve. By understanding the signs of greed and its impact, we can take steps to prevent unethical leadership and promote integrity in governance.

Chapter 2: The Greed Trap – When Leaders Lose Their Way

Greed in Action: Recognizing the Shift from Service to Selfishness

Leadership, at its core, is about serving others. However, the allure of power, wealth, and status can sometimes cause leaders to stray from their original purpose. Greed, defined as an intense and selfish desire for something, especially wealth or power, is one of the most dangerous forces that can corrupt leadership.

Greed often starts subtly, manifesting as small shifts in priorities. A leader who once focused on the needs of the community may begin prioritizing personal gain or the interests of a select few over the greater good. Over time, these small compromises can evolve into significant ethical lapses.

Identifying when a leader is slipping into the greed trap is crucial for preventing further damage. Warning signs include a lack of transparency, growing distance from the public, an obsession with personal image, and a tendency to dismiss or suppress dissenting voices. Leaders who act out of greed often make decisions that benefit themselves or their inner circle rather than the people they are supposed to serve.

Case Studies of Corruption: Real-World Examples of Greedy Leadership

Throughout history, many leaders have fallen into the greed trap, leading to disastrous consequences for their communities and nations. Understanding these real-world cases can help us recognize similar patterns in current and future leaders.

1. The Fall of Enron:
Enron was once one of the largest energy companies in the world, hailed for its innovation and rapid growth. However, behind the scenes, its leaders were engaging in massive fraud, manipulating financial statements to hide the company's mounting debts while inflating profits. The greed-driven actions of Enron's top executives ultimately led to the company's collapse in 2001, resulting in the loss of thousands of jobs and billions of dollars for investors. This scandal also led to the dissolution of Arthur Andersen, one of the world's largest accounting firms, which had been complicit in the fraud.

2. The Downfall of Richard Nixon:
The Watergate scandal of the early 1970s is another stark example of greed and corruption in leadership. President Richard Nixon and his administration engaged in illegal activities, including breaking into the Democratic National Committee headquarters and attempting to cover up their involvement. Nixon's desire to maintain power at all costs, driven by a sense of entitlement and greed, led to his resignation in 1974. The scandal severely damaged public trust in government and had long-lasting effects on American politics.

3. The Dictatorship of Ferdinand Marcos:
Ferdinand Marcos ruled the Philippines with an iron fist from 1965 to 1986. His regime was marked by widespread corruption, human rights abuses, and the embezzlement of billions of dollars from the country's coffers. Marcos and his wife, Imelda, lived in extravagant luxury while the majority of Filipinos lived in poverty. Their greed-fueled dictatorship led to economic decline, social unrest, and the eventual overthrow of Marcos during the People Power Revolution.

These examples illustrate the severe consequences of allowing greed to govern leadership decisions. In each case, the leaders involved prioritized their own interests over those of the people they were supposed to serve, leading to widespread suffering and, ultimately, their downfall.

The Impact on Us: How Greedy Leaders Hurt Communities

The repercussions of greedy leadership extend far beyond the personal gain of those in power. When leaders prioritize their interests over the needs of their constituents, entire communities suffer. The effects can be seen in various aspects of society, from economic inequality to social unrest and the erosion of democratic institutions.

1. Economic Inequality:
Greedy leaders often implement policies that disproportionately benefit the wealthy and powerful at the expense of the broader population. This leads to a widening gap between the rich and the poor, with those in power accumulating more wealth while the average citizen struggles to make ends meet. Such policies can include tax cuts for the wealthy, deregulation that favors large corporations, and cuts to social programs that support the most vulnerable.

2. Corruption and Misallocation of Resources:

When leaders are driven by greed, corruption often follows. Public funds meant for infrastructure, education, healthcare, and other essential services are diverted to personal accounts or used to secure political loyalty. This misallocation of resources undermines the development of communities and deprives citizens of the services they need to thrive.

3. Erosion of Trust in Government:

Perhaps one of the most damaging effects of greedy leadership is the erosion of public trust. When citizens see their leaders acting out of self-interest, they lose faith in the institutions meant to protect and serve them. This distrust can lead to apathy, disengagement from the political process, and, in extreme cases, the rise of populist or authoritarian movements that promise to "clean up" the system.

4. Social Unrest and Instability:

Greed-driven policies and actions often lead to social unrest. When people feel that their leaders are not acting in their best interest, they are more likely to protest, strike, or even revolt. Such instability can have long-lasting effects on a nation's social fabric, economy, and international standing.

Conclusion

Greed is a powerful and destructive force in leadership. It distorts decision-making, prioritizes personal gain over the public good, and ultimately leads to the downfall of leaders and the suffering of communities. Recognizing the signs of greed in leadership is essential for preventing corruption and ensuring that those in power are truly committed to serving the people.

As we move forward in this book, we will explore the traits of ethical leaders, how to identify them, and the role each of us can play in promoting and sustaining ethical governance. By understanding the dangers of greed and the importance of integrity, we can help shape a future where power is used to uplift communities rather than exploit them.

Chapter 3: Real Traits of Ethical Leaders – What We Should Look For

Integrity in Action: The Hallmarks of Honest Leadership

Integrity is the foundation of ethical leadership. It is the quality that ensures a leader's words and actions are aligned with moral principles and the best interests of the people they serve. An ethical leader acts with integrity even when no one is watching, making decisions based on what is right rather than what is easy or personally advantageous.

One of the most critical aspects of integrity is consistency. Ethical leaders are consistent in their values and actions, regardless of the situation or the audience. They don't change their stance on issues based on what is politically expedient or personally beneficial. Instead, they uphold their principles, demonstrating that their commitment to ethical behavior is genuine and unwavering.

Another hallmark of integrity is honesty. Ethical leaders communicate truthfully, even when the truth is uncomfortable or unpopular. They avoid deception and manipulation, choosing instead to build trust through transparency and openness. When leaders are honest, they create an environment where trust can flourish, and this trust becomes the bedrock of their leadership.

A key indicator of integrity is a leader's willingness to admit mistakes and take responsibility for their actions. Ethical leaders understand that no one is perfect, and they don't shy away from acknowledging when they've made a wrong decision. They don't deflect blame or make excuses; instead, they learn from their mistakes and use those lessons to improve their leadership.

Transparency and Trust: Why Open Leaders Build Stronger Societies

Transparency is another vital trait of ethical leadership. It involves being open about one's actions, decisions, and motivations, and ensuring that the processes of governance are clear and accessible to the public. Transparency is essential because it fosters trust, and trust is the glue that holds societies together.

Leaders who operate transparently invite scrutiny and are willing to be held accountable for their decisions. This openness allows citizens to understand how decisions are made, why certain policies are implemented, and how public funds are used. When leaders are transparent, they reduce the risk of corruption and increase public confidence in their governance.

Transparency is also about communication. Ethical leaders ensure that their communications with the public are clear, truthful, and timely. They don't withhold critical information or mislead the public to avoid controversy. Instead, they engage with citizens openly, providing the information necessary for the public to make informed decisions.

One of the most significant benefits of transparency is that it builds trust between leaders and the people they serve. When citizens trust their leaders, they are more likely to support their policies and work together towards common goals. Trust also makes it easier for leaders to navigate crises and implement necessary changes, as the public is more likely to cooperate when they believe their leaders are acting in good faith.

In contrast, a lack of transparency breeds suspicion and distrust. When leaders are secretive or deceptive, it creates a sense of unease among the public, leading to disillusionment and disengagement. This erosion of trust can have long-lasting consequences, making it difficult for leaders to effectively govern and for societies to thrive.

Making a Difference: How Ethical Leaders Impact Real Lives

Ethical leadership is not just about avoiding wrongdoing; it's about actively making a positive difference in the lives of others. Ethical leaders are driven by a genuine desire to serve their communities and improve the well-being of the people they represent. This commitment to service is reflected in the decisions they make, the policies they implement, and the way they interact with others.

One of the most significant impacts of ethical leadership is the creation of more just and equitable societies. Ethical leaders work to ensure that all members of the community have access to the resources and opportunities they need to succeed. They are committed to fairness and strive to eliminate inequalities that prevent people from reaching their full potential.

Ethical leaders also prioritize the long-term well-being of their communities. They make decisions that are sustainable and consider the future impacts of their actions. Whether it's protecting the environment, investing in education, or fostering economic development, ethical leaders focus on creating a legacy of positive change that will benefit future generations.

Moreover, ethical leaders empower others. They encourage participation, listen to diverse perspectives, and foster a sense of ownership among community members. By involving people in the decision-making process and respecting their input, ethical leaders create a more inclusive and democratic society.

The impact of ethical leadership is also evident in the level of trust and cooperation within a community. When people believe their leaders are acting in their best interests, they are more likely to work together, support one another, and contribute to the common good. This sense of community and mutual support is a direct result of ethical leadership and is essential for the health and vitality of any society.

Conclusion

Ethical leadership is defined by integrity, transparency, and a commitment to making a positive difference in the lives of others. Leaders who embody these traits not only avoid the pitfalls of greed and corruption but also actively contribute to the well-being and progress of their communities. By recognizing these qualities in leaders, we can better identify those who are truly committed to serving the public good and making a lasting impact.

As we move forward in this book, we will explore how to identify and evaluate leaders based on these traits, and how to ensure that those in power are held accountable to the highest ethical standards. By doing so, we can help create a future where leadership is guided by principles of fairness, justice, and integrity.

Chapter 4: Seeing Through the Lies – Identifying Greedy Leaders

Spotting Red Flags: The Warning Signs of Self-Interest in Leadership

Identifying greedy leaders is crucial for safeguarding the integrity of our communities and ensuring that those in power are genuinely committed to serving the public good. Greedy leaders often disguise their self-serving motives behind appealing rhetoric and public displays of concern, making it challenging to see through the façade. However, there are several red flags that can indicate a leader's underlying greed and self-interest.

1. Lack of Transparency:
Greedy leaders tend to operate in secrecy, withholding important information from the public or making decisions behind closed doors. They may resist efforts to increase transparency, such as open meetings, public records requests, or financial disclosures. A leader who avoids scrutiny and refuses to provide clear explanations for their actions may be hiding unethical behavior or conflicts of interest.

2. Inconsistent Behavior and Flip-Flopping:
Greedy leaders often change their positions on key issues depending on what benefits them the most at any given time. This inconsistency can be a sign that they are more interested in maintaining power or gaining financial rewards than in serving their constituents. Watch for leaders who frequently shift their stances, particularly if these changes align with the interests of powerful donors or special interest groups.

3. Excessive Focus on Personal Image:
Leaders who are overly concerned with their public image or who engage in constant self-promotion may be more interested in advancing their careers than in addressing the needs of the people they serve. This focus on personal branding can manifest in frequent media appearances, lavish spending on personal projects, or a relentless pursuit of accolades and recognition.

4. Prioritizing Wealthy Donors and Special Interests:
Pay attention to where a leader's support comes from. If they rely heavily on contributions from wealthy donors, corporations, or special interest groups, there's

a strong possibility that their policies will favor these entities over the general public. Greedy leaders often prioritize the interests of those who fund their campaigns or offer them personal benefits, leading to policies that disproportionately benefit the wealthy and powerful.

5. Resistance to Accountability:
Greedy leaders frequently resist efforts to hold them accountable, whether through legal means, public oversight, or internal checks and balances. They may attack or undermine watchdog groups, the media, or political opponents who challenge their actions. This resistance to accountability is a clear indication that a leader is more interested in protecting their power than in being transparent and responsible.

6. Conflict of Interest:
Leaders who have significant financial interests in businesses, industries, or policies that they can influence through their official duties are at high risk of acting out of greed. Watch for situations where a leader stands to gain personally from a decision they are involved in making. Failure to divest from conflicting interests or to disclose potential conflicts is a major red flag.

Real-World Comparisons: Examples of Ethical vs. Greedy Leadership

To better understand the contrast between ethical and greedy leadership, it is helpful to examine real-world examples. These case studies highlight the differences in behavior, decision-making, and outcomes between leaders who prioritize the common good and those driven by self-interest.

Example 1: Ethical Leadership - Nelson Mandela
Nelson Mandela is celebrated as a model of ethical leadership. Throughout his life, Mandela consistently prioritized the welfare of his people over his personal gain. Despite suffering 27 years of imprisonment, he emerged as a leader committed to reconciliation, justice, and equality. Mandela's leadership was marked by transparency, accountability, and a deep commitment to the principles of democracy. He rejected the trappings of power, choosing instead to focus on healing a divided nation and creating opportunities for all South Africans.

Example 2: Greedy Leadership - Robert Mugabe
In stark contrast, Robert Mugabe's leadership in Zimbabwe is a cautionary tale of greed and corruption. Initially seen as a liberation hero, Mugabe's rule became increasingly autocratic and self-serving over time. He amassed personal wealth

while the country's economy collapsed, and his policies led to widespread poverty and repression. Mugabe manipulated elections, silenced opposition, and prioritized his own power and wealth over the well-being of the Zimbabwean people. His legacy is one of economic ruin, social division, and international isolation.

Example 3: Ethical Leadership - Angela Merkel

Angela Merkel, the former Chancellor of Germany, is another example of ethical leadership. Known for her pragmatic and thoughtful approach, Merkel consistently made decisions based on what she believed was best for Germany and Europe, even when those decisions were politically unpopular. Her leadership during the Eurozone crisis and the refugee crisis was characterized by a commitment to humanitarian values, transparency, and careful consideration of long-term impacts. Merkel's leadership style emphasized accountability and integrity, earning her respect both domestically and internationally.

Example 4: Greedy Leadership - Ferdinand Marcos

Ferdinand Marcos, the former president of the Philippines, exemplified greedy leadership. His regime was marked by massive corruption, human rights abuses, and the plundering of the country's wealth. Marcos and his wife, Imelda, lived in opulence while the majority of Filipinos suffered under economic hardship. The couple embezzled billions of dollars from public funds, and their greed left a lasting scar on the Philippines, contributing to ongoing economic and political challenges long after their rule ended.

These examples illustrate the stark differences between leaders who act out of ethical principles and those who are driven by greed. Ethical leaders like Mandela and Merkel are remembered for their contributions to peace, justice, and prosperity, while greedy leaders like Mugabe and Marcos are known for the harm they caused and the trust they betrayed.

Tools for Today: Practical Ways to Evaluate Leaders in Your Community

Evaluating the ethical qualities of leaders is a crucial skill for any engaged citizen. While it can be challenging to see through the carefully crafted public images of politicians and officials, there are practical tools and strategies that can help you assess whether a leader is likely to act ethically or out of self-interest.

1. Research Their Background:

Start by investigating a leader's history. Look at their career path, past decisions, and any patterns of behavior that may indicate a predisposition towards ethical or greedy behavior. Examine their financial history, connections to businesses or industries, and any previous instances of misconduct.

2.Analyze Their Policy Proposals:

Pay close attention to the policies that a leader advocates for. Are these policies designed to benefit the community as a whole, or do they disproportionately favor a select few? Consider who stands to gain the most from these proposals and whether the leader's actions align with their stated values.

3.Observe Their Communication Style:

How a leader communicates can provide insights into their ethical standards. Leaders who are transparent, open to criticism, and willing to engage in honest dialogue are more likely to act ethically. On the other hand, those who evade questions, deflect blame, or attack their critics may be hiding unethical behavior.

4.Examine Their Financial Disclosures:

Many countries require politicians and public officials to disclose their financial interests. Reviewing these disclosures can help you identify potential conflicts of interest. Be wary of leaders who have significant investments in industries they can influence or who receive large donations from special interest groups.

5.Consider Their Accountability Measures:

Ethical leaders often put in place mechanisms to hold themselves accountable, such as independent audits, regular public reports, or open meetings. Evaluate whether a leader welcomes oversight and accountability or if they resist it.

6.Engage With Independent Media and Watchdog Organizations:

Independent journalists and watchdog groups play a crucial role in uncovering corruption and unethical behavior. Follow their reports to gain a more nuanced understanding of a leader's actions and motivations. These organizations can provide valuable context and evidence that may not be available through mainstream media or official channels.

Conclusion

Identifying greedy leaders is not always straightforward, but by staying vigilant and using the tools outlined in this chapter, you can better protect your community from the dangers of unethical leadership. Recognizing the red flags, comparing real-world examples, and critically evaluating those in power are all essential steps in ensuring that leadership serves the public good rather than personal gain.

As we continue in this book, we will explore the role of communities in shaping leadership and how collective action can promote and sustain ethical governance. By working together, we can create a future where leaders are chosen for their integrity, transparency, and commitment to the well-being of all.

Chapter 5: Our Role in Shaping Leadership – The Power of Community Action

Creating a Culture of Accountability: How Communities Can Demand Better

Ethical leadership doesn't just happen by chance—it's often the result of a community that actively fosters and demands integrity from its leaders. Communities have a tremendous capacity to influence the type of leadership they receive by creating a culture of accountability, transparency, and participation. When citizens are engaged and proactive, they can set the standards for what they expect from those in power.

One of the most effective ways for a community to encourage ethical leadership is through civic education. By ensuring that citizens are informed about their rights, the responsibilities of leaders, and the workings of government, communities can create a more engaged and knowledgeable electorate. Education empowers individuals to make informed decisions, hold leaders accountable, and participate effectively in the democratic process.

Communities can also promote ethical leadership by establishing clear expectations and norms around transparency and accountability. This can be done through community organizations, local media, and public forums where leaders are encouraged—or required—to share information about their decisions, financial interests, and policy goals. When transparency is the norm, it becomes more difficult for unethical behavior to go unnoticed or unchallenged.

Finally, fostering a culture of active participation is crucial. When citizens regularly engage with their leaders, whether through voting, attending town hall meetings, or participating in public consultations, it sends a clear message that the community is invested in ethical governance. Leaders who know that their actions are being closely watched and that they are accountable to an informed and active electorate are more likely to act with integrity.

The Strength of Civic Engagement: Real Stories of Change from the Ground Up

Civic engagement is the cornerstone of any vibrant democracy, and history is full of examples where communities have come together to demand better leadership and effect meaningful change. These stories illustrate the power of collective action and the impact that engaged citizens can have on their communities.

1. The Civil Rights Movement in the United States:

One of the most powerful examples of civic engagement is the Civil Rights Movement of the 1950s and 1960s. Faced with systemic racism and inequality, African Americans and their allies organized mass protests, boycotts, and legal challenges to demand equal rights. Leaders like Dr. Martin Luther King Jr. emerged from this movement, driven by a commitment to justice and ethical leadership. The sustained efforts of engaged citizens led to significant legislative changes, including the Civil Rights Act of 1964 and the Voting Rights Act of 1965, which transformed American society and expanded the promise of democracy to millions.

2. The Anti-Corruption Movement in India:

In India, the anti-corruption movement led by activist Anna Hazare in 2011 is another example of the power of civic engagement. Frustrated by widespread corruption in government, millions of Indians took to the streets to demand greater transparency and accountability from their leaders. The movement galvanized public opinion and led to the passage of the Lokpal and Lokayuktas Act in 2013, which established an independent anti-corruption ombudsman. This movement demonstrated the potential of collective action to bring about institutional change and hold leaders accountable.

3. The Arab Spring:

The Arab Spring, which began in 2010, saw a wave of pro-democracy uprisings across the Middle East and North Africa. Citizens in countries like Tunisia, Egypt, and Libya demanded an end to authoritarian regimes and the establishment of democratic governance. Although the outcomes of these uprisings were varied, the Arab Spring underscored the power of civic engagement and the desire of people across the region to live under leadership that respects human rights and operates with integrity.

4. The Anti-Apartheid Movement in South Africa:

The struggle against apartheid in South Africa is another testament to the power of civic engagement. For decades, South Africans of all races resisted the racist policies of the apartheid regime through protests, strikes, and international advocacy. Leaders like Nelson Mandela, Desmond Tutu, and others inspired a global movement that ultimately led to the dismantling of apartheid and the establishment of a democratic government in 1994. This movement demonstrated that sustained civic engagement could overcome even the most entrenched systems of oppression.

These examples highlight the transformative potential of civic engagement. When communities come together to demand ethical leadership, they can challenge the status quo, bring about systemic change, and create a more just and equitable society. Civic engagement empowers individuals to take control of their destinies and hold leaders to the highest standards of accountability and integrity.

Keeping Leaders in Check: Effective Strategies for Ensuring Responsibility

Holding leaders accountable is a continuous process that requires vigilance and active participation from the community. Even the most well-intentioned leaders can fall prey to the temptations of power, which is why it is essential to have systems and strategies in place to ensure that they remain responsible to the people they serve.

1. Regular and Transparent Communication:

One of the most effective ways to keep leaders accountable is by establishing regular and transparent channels of communication between the government and the public. Town hall meetings, public forums, and online platforms can provide opportunities for citizens to ask questions, express concerns, and receive updates from their leaders. Transparency fosters trust and allows citizens to stay informed about the decisions being made on their behalf.

2. Independent Media and Investigative Journalism:

A free and independent press is crucial for holding leaders accountable. Investigative journalism plays a vital role in uncovering corruption, exposing unethical behavior, and providing citizens with the information they need to make informed decisions. Supporting local and independent media outlets, subscribing to credible news sources, and sharing verified information can help ensure that leaders are subject to scrutiny and that the public remains aware of their actions.

3. Legal and Institutional Oversight:

Legal frameworks and institutions designed to monitor and check the power of leaders are essential for maintaining accountability. This includes independent judiciary bodies, anti-corruption commissions, and ombudsman offices. Citizens can support these institutions by advocating for their independence, funding, and authority to investigate and prosecute unethical behavior. Engaging in public campaigns to strengthen these oversight mechanisms is a powerful way to ensure that leaders remain accountable.

4. Public Protests and Advocacy:
When leaders fail to respond to the needs and concerns of the community, public protests and advocacy campaigns can be effective tools for demanding accountability. Peaceful demonstrations, petitions, and social media campaigns can draw attention to issues, mobilize public support, and pressure leaders to change course or step down if necessary. Advocacy groups and non-governmental organizations (NGOs) can also play a critical role in organizing and sustaining these efforts.

5. Electoral Accountability:
Voting is one of the most direct ways to hold leaders accountable. By participating in elections and supporting candidates who demonstrate a commitment to ethical leadership, citizens can ensure that those in power are held responsible for their actions. It's essential to remain engaged in the electoral process, from local elections to national contests, and to advocate for free, fair, and transparent voting systems.

Conclusion
Communities have immense power to shape the quality of leadership they receive. By fostering a culture of civic engagement, transparency, and accountability, citizens can ensure that their leaders act with integrity and prioritize the common good. The examples of successful civic movements around the world demonstrate that when people come together to demand ethical leadership, they can achieve significant and lasting change.

As we move forward, it is important to remember that ethical leadership is not just the responsibility of those in power—it is a collective effort that involves everyone. By staying informed, participating in the political process, and holding leaders accountable, we can help create a future where leadership is guided by principles of fairness, justice, and integrity.

In the next chapter, we will explore the real-world impacts of leadership choices, examining how ethical and unethical leadership has shaped communities and societies over time. By understanding these impacts, we can better appreciate the importance of promoting and supporting ethical leaders.

Chapter 6: The Real-World Impacts of Leadership Choices

Stories of Success and Failure in Leadership

Leadership decisions have a profound and lasting impact on communities, nations, and the world. Throughout history, the choices made by leaders have led to either the upliftment or the downfall of societies. In this chapter, we will explore real-world examples of both successful and failed leadership, highlighting the significant consequences that stem from ethical and unethical decision-making.

Success Story: The New Deal and Franklin D. Roosevelt

One of the most iconic examples of successful leadership is Franklin D. Roosevelt's New Deal, a series of programs and policies implemented in the United States during the 1930s to combat the Great Depression. Faced with widespread unemployment, economic instability, and social unrest, Roosevelt took bold and decisive action to address the crisis.

The New Deal included initiatives such as Social Security, unemployment insurance, and public works projects that provided jobs to millions of Americans. Roosevelt's leadership was characterized by a commitment to the common good, empathy for those suffering, and a willingness to challenge the status quo. His decisions not only helped the United States recover from the Great Depression but also laid the foundation for a more equitable society.

Roosevelt's leadership during this period is remembered as a success because it demonstrated the positive impact of ethical decision-making. By prioritizing the needs of the people over political expediency, Roosevelt was able to restore public confidence, stimulate economic growth, and create lasting social safety nets that continue to benefit Americans today.

Failure Story: The Collapse of Enron

In contrast, the collapse of Enron in 2001 serves as a stark example of the catastrophic consequences of unethical leadership. Enron, once one of the largest energy companies in the world, was brought down by a culture of greed, deception, and corruption at the highest levels of the company.

Enron's executives engaged in widespread accounting fraud, using complex finacial schemes to hide the company's debt and inflate profits. They prioritized short-term gains and personal enrichment over the long-term health of the company and the well-being of their employees and shareholders. When the fraud was eventually exposed, Enron quickly spiraled into bankruptcy, wiping out the savings of thousands of employees and investors.

The collapse of Enron not only led to significant financial losses but also damaged public trust in corporate governance and the financial markets. The scandal resulted in increased regulatory scrutiny and the passage of new laws aimed at preventing similar abuses in the future. Enron's failure is a cautionary tale of what happens when leaders abandon ethics in pursuit of personal gain.

Success Story: The Reconciliation Process in South Africa

Another powerful example of successful leadership is the reconciliation process led by Nelson Mandela in South Africa. After decades of apartheid, a brutal system of racial segregation and oppression, South Africa was on the brink of civil war. Mandela, who had spent 27 years in prison for his anti-apartheid activism, emerged as a leader committed to peace, reconciliation, and nation-building.

Rather than seeking revenge against those who had upheld apartheid, Mandela chose to pursue a path of forgiveness and unity. He established the Truth and Reconciliation Commission, which allowed victims of apartheid to share their stories and perpetrators to confess their crimes in exchange for amnesty. This process helped South Africa transition to a multiracial democracy without descending into further violence.

Mandela's leadership is celebrated as a success because it demonstrated the power of ethical decision-making in healing a divided nation. By prioritizing reconciliation over retribution, Mandela was able to bring together a deeply fractured society and lay the groundwork for a more inclusive and just South Africa.

Failure Story: The Rwandan Genocide

The Rwandan Genocide of 1994 is one of the most tragic examples of failed leadership in recent history. Over the course of just 100 days, an estimated 800,000 Tutsis and moderate Hutus were slaughtered by extremist Hutu militias, with the tacit approval and sometimes active participation of the Rwandan government.

The genocide was the result of years of ethnic tension, propaganda, and the failure of the Rwandan leadership to prevent or stop the violence. Instead of promoting unity and peace, the government fueled hatred and division, encouraging the mass killing of innocent civilians. The international community also failed to act decisively to stop the genocide, leading to one of the worst humanitarian crises of the 20th century.

The Rwandan Genocide is a stark reminder of the devastating consequences of unethical leadership. When leaders prioritize power, ideology, or ethnic supremacy over the well-being of their people, the results can be catastrophic. The genocide left a deep scar on Rwanda and the world, underscoring the importance of ethical leadership in preventing such atrocities.

The Long-Term Effects of Ethical vs. Unethical Leadership

The stories of success and failure in leadership illustrate the long-term effects that leadership choices can have on societies. Ethical leadership can lead to positive outcomes that resonate for generations, while unethical leadership can cause lasting harm and suffering.

Ethical Leadership and Its Lasting Impact

Ethical leadership, as demonstrated by figures like Franklin D. Roosevelt and Nelson Mandela, creates a legacy of trust, stability, and progress. When leaders act with integrity, transparency, and a commitment to the common good, they inspire confidence and cooperation among their followers. This, in turn, leads to more resilient societies that are better equipped to face challenges and adapt to change.

The long-term effects of ethical leadership include:
- **Social Cohesion:** Ethical leaders work to bridge divides and bring people together, fostering a sense of community and shared purpose.
- **Economic Stability:** By prioritizing sustainable policies and practices, ethical leaders can promote economic growth that benefits all members of society, not just the wealthy few.
- **Public Trust:** Ethical leaders earn the trust of their constituents, which is essential for the effective functioning of government and society.
- **Legacy of Justice**: Ethical leadership often leaves a legacy of fairness, equality, and justice that continues to shape societies long after the leader has left office.

Unethical Leadership and Its Devastating Consequences

In contrast, unethical leadership, as seen in the examples of Enron and the Rwandan Genocide, leaves a legacy of distrust, division, and destruction. Leaders who act out of greed, self-interest, or malice often create conditions that lead to instability, conflict, and suffering.

The long-term effects of unethical leadership include:

- **Social Fragmentation:** Unethical leaders often exploit divisions within society, leading to increased polarization and conflict.
- **Economic Collapse:** When leaders prioritize short-term gains over long-term stability, they can cause economic crises that devastate communities and erode public confidence in institutions.
- **Erosion of Trust:** Unethical behavior by leaders undermines public trust, making it difficult for future leaders to govern effectively and for society to function smoothly.
- **Legacy of Injustice:** Unethical leadership often perpetuates systems of inequality and injustice, creating enduring harm that can take generations to repair.

Conclusion

The choices made by leaders have far-reaching consequences that extend well beyond their time in office. Ethical leadership can uplift societies, creating lasting legacies of justice, trust, and prosperity. In contrast, unethical leadership can lead to division, suffering, and destruction that reverberates through generations.

As citizens, it is our responsibility to support and demand ethical leadership. By understanding the real-world impacts of leadership choices, we can better appreciate the importance of integrity, transparency, and accountability in those who hold power. In the next chapter, we will explore practical steps for choosing ethical leaders and how we, as individuals and communities, can play a role in shaping the future of our society.

Chapter 7: How to Choose Leaders Who Won't Let Us Down

Doing Your Homework: How to Research and Understand Candidates

Choosing ethical leaders starts with being an informed voter. In a world where political campaigns are often saturated with sound bites, slogans, and flashy advertisements, it's easy to be swayed by superficial impressions. However, making an informed decision requires digging deeper into the backgrounds, policies, and character of the candidates. This chapter will guide you through the process of researching and understanding candidates to ensure that you are making a choice that aligns with your values and the best interests of your community.

Step 1: Investigate the Candidate's Background

A candidate's history can provide significant insights into their character, decision-making style, and potential for ethical leadership. Here's how to start:

- **Educational and Professional Background:** Examine the candidate's education and career history. Does their background demonstrate a commitment to public service or community involvement? Have they held positions that required ethical decision-making or leadership? While education and experience alone don't determine ethical behavior, they can provide context for understanding a candidate's values and priorities.
- **Previous Political Experience:** If the candidate has held office before, review their record. How did they vote on key issues? Were they involved in any scandals or controversies? Look for patterns in their behavior—consistent support for ethical policies, transparency, and accountability is a good sign.
- **Financial Interests and Donors:** Research the candidate's financial interests and campaign donors. Are there potential conflicts of interest? Candidates heavily funded by special interest groups or corporations may be more inclined to prioritize those donors over the public good. Financial transparency is crucial, so look for candidates who openly disclose their financial ties.

Step 2: Analyze Their Policy Proposals

Understanding a candidate's policy positions is essential for determining whether they align with your values and the needs of your community. Here's what to consider:

- **Clarity and Feasibility:** Are the candidate's policy proposals clear and well-articulated? Do they provide specifics on how they will implement their plans, or are they vague and filled with platitudes? A well-thought-out policy platform indicates that the candidate has put serious effort into understanding the issues and finding practical solutions.
- **Alignment with Public Interest:** Evaluate whether the policies prioritize the common good over special interests. For example, does the candidate support healthcare access, educational opportunities, and environmental protection? Ethical leaders advocate for policies that benefit the majority, particularly those who are most vulnerable.
- **Consistency with Past Actions:** Compare the candidate's current policy proposals with their past actions. Have they demonstrated a commitment to these issues throughout their career, or is this a recent shift? Consistency in policy positions is a strong indicator of genuine commitment, rather than opportunism.

Step 3: Observe Their Communication Style

How a candidate communicates can reveal much about their character and leadership style. Here's what to watch for:

- **Openness and Honesty:** Does the candidate communicate openly and honestly with voters? Ethical leaders are transparent about their intentions, policies, and decisions. Look for candidates who are willing to answer tough questions, admit mistakes, and engage in meaningful dialogue with constituents.
- **Respect for Opponents and Constituents:** Pay attention to how the candidate treats others, including their opponents and those who disagree with them. Ethical leaders show respect, even in the face of criticism. Avoid candidates who rely on negative campaigning, personal attacks, or divisive rhetoric.
- **Engagement with the Public:** Does the candidate make an effort to engage with the public? Do they hold town hall meetings, respond to questions on social media, or participate in community events? Leaders who actively seek out and listen to the concerns of their constituents are more likely to be responsive and accountable once in office.

Making Your Voice Count: The Reality of Voting and Participation

Voting is one of the most powerful tools citizens have to influence the direction of their community and country. However, simply casting a ballot is not enough; informed and strategic voting is key to ensuring that ethical leaders are elected. Here's how to make your vote count:

Understanding the Electoral Process

First, familiarize yourself with the electoral process in your area. This includes understanding the different types of elections (local, state, national), how often they occur, and the rules for voter registration and voting. Knowing the process helps ensure that you are prepared and that your vote is cast and counted correctly.

- **Local Elections:** These often include city council members, mayors, school board members, and other local officials. While these elections may seem less significant than national ones, the leaders chosen at the local level have a direct and immediate impact on your daily life.
- **State Elections:** These include governors, state legislators, and other state officials. State governments play a critical role in shaping policies on education, healthcare, transportation, and more.
- **National Elections:** These include elections for the president, senators, and representatives. National leaders set the overall direction of the country and make decisions that affect all citizens.

Voting Strategically

Strategic voting involves thinking about both short-term and long-term outcomes. Here are some strategies:

- **Vote with Your Values:** Focus on candidates who align with your core values, especially when it comes to integrity, transparency, and accountability. Even if a candidate doesn't align with you on every issue, prioritizing ethics in leadership can lead to better governance overall.
- **Consider the Bigger Picture:** Sometimes, it's necessary to vote for a candidate who has the best chance of winning against a less ethical opponent, even if they are not your ideal choice. This is particularly relevant in closely contested races where the stakes are high.
- **Support Down-Ballot Candidates:** Don't overlook the importance of down-ballot races (local and state elections). These officials play crucial roles in implementing and enforcing laws, and they can often have more direct influence on your community than national figures.
- **Stay Engaged Beyond Elections:** Voting is just the beginning. Stay engaged by following up on the actions of those you've elected, participating in community meetings, and advocating for policies that align with your values.

Building a Movement: Organizing Communities for Ethical Leadership

While individual actions like voting are crucial, collective action can amplify the impact and lead to more significant change. Here's how to organize your community to support ethical leadership:

Step 1: Form or Join a Community Group
Creating or joining a community group focused on ethical leadership can help pool resources, share information, and mobilize voters. These groups can be formal organizations or informal networks of like-minded individuals.

- **Focus on Education:** Ensure that members of your group are informed about the candidates, issues, and voting process. Host educational events, distribute informational materials, and use social media to spread awareness.
- **Engage with Local Media:** Write op-eds, letters to the editor, or work with local journalists to highlight the importance of ethical leadership in your community. Media coverage can raise awareness and influence public opinion.

Step 2: Mobilize Voters
Turnout is often a deciding factor in elections, so mobilizing voters is critical. Here's how:

- **Get Out the Vote (GOTV) Campaigns:** Organize GOTV efforts to remind people to vote, provide information on polling locations, and offer assistance with transportation to the polls.
- **Canvassing and Phone Banking:** Direct outreach through door-to-door canvassing or phone banking can make a significant difference, particularly in local elections. Personal contact is one of the most effective ways to encourage people to vote.
- **Use Social Media:** Social media platforms are powerful tools for organizing and mobilizing. Use them to share important information, connect with other voters, and create a sense of community around the election.

Step 3: Hold Elected Officials Accountable
Once the election is over, the work of ensuring ethical leadership continues. Here's how to keep elected officials accountable:

- **Monitor Their Actions:** Follow the actions of elected officials closely. Pay attention to how they vote, the policies they support, and whether they fulfill their campaign promises.
- **Engage in Advocacy:** If elected officials stray from their commitments or engage in unethical behavior, organize advocacy efforts to demand accountability. This could include petitions, public protests, or working with watchdog organizations.
- **Support Recalls or Challenges:** In extreme cases where an elected official engages in serious misconduct, work with your community to support a recall election or to challenge their re-election bid.

Conclusion

Choosing ethical leaders is one of the most important responsibilities we have as citizens. By doing your homework, voting strategically, and organizing your community, you can help ensure that the leaders who are elected are those who will serve with integrity, transparency, and a commitment to the common good.

Leadership is a reflection of the values and priorities of the people who choose it. By actively participating in the electoral process and demanding accountability from our leaders, we can build a society where ethical leadership is not just an aspiration, but a reality. In the next chapter, we will explore the future of leadership and how emerging trends and challenges will shape the leaders of tomorrow.

Chapter 8: The Changing Landscape – What's Next for Leadership?

Adapting to Change: How Modern Challenges Are Redefining Leadership

The world is rapidly evolving, and with it, the demands and expectations of leadership are changing. In this era of unprecedented technological advancements, global interconnectedness, and shifting social dynamics, leaders face new challenges that require them to be more adaptable, innovative, and ethically grounded than ever before. This chapter explores how modern challenges are redefining leadership and what qualities are essential for future leaders.

The Impact of Globalization

Globalization has transformed the way societies interact, trade, and communicate. While it has brought about economic growth and cross-cultural exchange, it has also introduced new complexities for leaders to navigate. Globalization has made national boundaries less significant, meaning that decisions made by leaders in one country can have far-reaching consequences across the globe.

Challenges for Leaders:

- **Economic Interdependence:** Leaders must balance the interests of their nation with the demands of a global economy. This requires a deep understanding of international trade, finance, and regulation, as well as the ability to negotiate and collaborate with other nations.
- **Cultural Sensitivity:** As societies become more diverse and interconnected, leaders must be culturally aware and sensitive to the needs and values of different communities. This involves promoting inclusivity, understanding cultural nuances, and fostering cooperation across cultural divides.
- **Global Crises:** Issues such as climate change, pandemics, and international conflicts require leaders who can think globally while acting locally. Addressing these challenges demands a collaborative approach that goes beyond national interests to consider the well-being of the entire planet.

The Rise of Populism

In recent years, populism has emerged as a powerful force in global politics. Populist leaders often position themselves as champions of the "common people" against a perceived elite, using rhetoric that appeals to emotions and identity rather than policy and reason. While populism can energize and mobilize certain segments of the population, it also poses significant risks to democratic institutions and social cohesion.

Challenges for Leaders:
- **Maintaining Integrity:** Populist movements can tempt leaders to prioritize short-term popularity over long-term governance. Ethical leaders must resist the urge to engage in divisive rhetoric or exploit societal fears for political gain.
- **Upholding Democratic Norms:** Populist leaders often challenge established norms and institutions, leading to potential erosion of democratic checks and balances. Future leaders must be committed to protecting these institutions and ensuring that power is exercised responsibly.
- **Bridging Divides:** Populism can exacerbate divisions within society, pitting different groups against each other. Leaders must focus on uniting rather than dividing, fostering dialogue and understanding between disparate communities.

The Role of Technology and Social Media
Technology and social media have revolutionized the way leaders communicate with the public and how citizens engage with politics. While these tools have the potential to enhance transparency and participation, they also come with significant challenges, including the spread of misinformation, cyber threats, and the erosion of privacy.

Challenges for Leaders:
- **Combating Misinformation:** The rise of social media has made it easier for misinformation to spread rapidly, often outpacing efforts to correct it. Leaders must be vigilant in promoting accurate information and countering falsehoods, while also respecting freedom of expression.
- **Ensuring Cybersecurity:** As governments, businesses, and individuals become more reliant on digital technology, cybersecurity has become a critical concern. Leaders must prioritize the protection of sensitive information and infrastructure from cyber threats, including state-sponsored attacks and cybercrime.
- **Navigating Digital Ethics:** The ethical implications of technology, from data privacy to artificial intelligence, require leaders who are knowledgeable and forward-thinking. They must strike a balance between embracing technological innovation and safeguarding individual rights and societal values.

Climate Change and Environmental Stewardship
Climate change represents one of the most pressing challenges facing current and future leaders. The impacts of global warming—rising sea levels, extreme weather events, loss of biodiversity—are already being felt worldwide. Addressing this crisis requires bold and decisive action at both the local and global levels.

Challenges for Leaders:
- **Sustainable Development:** Leaders must integrate sustainability into all aspects of governance, from energy policy to urban planning. This involves making difficult decisions that may challenge economic interests but are necessary for long-term environmental health.
- **Global Cooperation:** Climate change is a global issue that demands collective action. Leaders must be willing to cooperate with other nations, share resources and technology, and commit to international agreements that aim to reduce carbon emissions and protect the environment.
- **Climate Justice:** The effects of climate change are disproportionately felt by vulnerable communities, particularly in developing countries. Ethical leaders must advocate for climate justice, ensuring that the burdens of climate action do not fall unfairly on those least responsible for the crisis.

Vigilance is Key: Staying Involved in an Ever-Changing World
In a world characterized by rapid change and increasing complexity, staying informed and engaged is more important than ever. Ethical leadership depends not only on those in positions of power but also on the active participation of citizens. Here's how you can stay involved and help shape the future of leadership.

Continuous Learning and Adaptation
The challenges of tomorrow may differ significantly from those of today. To effectively contribute to the political process and hold leaders accountable, citizens must commit to continuous learning and adaptation.
- **Stay Informed:** Regularly seek out reliable news sources and educate yourself on current events, emerging trends, and global issues. Understanding the broader context of political decisions will help you make informed choices and advocate for meaningful change.
- **Engage in Public Discourse:** Participate in discussions about leadership and policy, whether online or in person. Engaging with others allows you to exchange ideas, challenge assumptions, and broaden your perspectives.

Advocacy and Activism
Even when the right leaders are in place, advocacy and activism remain essential for ensuring that their policies reflect the will of the people and that they remain accountable.

- **Support Causes You Believe In:** Whether it's through volunteering, donating, or simply raising awareness, find ways to support the causes that matter to you. This not only contributes to positive change but also encourages leaders to prioritize these issues.
- **Organize and Mobilize:** Use your voice to organize campaigns, petitions, or community events that bring attention to important issues. Mobilizing others amplifies your impact and sends a clear message to leaders that certain issues cannot be ignored.

Holding Leaders Accountable
As the world changes, so too must the methods by which we hold our leaders accountable. Traditional forms of accountability, such as voting and public scrutiny, remain vital, but new challenges require innovative approaches.

- **Digital Tools for Accountability:** Leverage technology to monitor the actions of leaders, track their voting records, and hold them accountable for their promises. Websites, apps, and social media platforms can be powerful tools for transparency and engagement.
- **Participate in Civic Activities:** Attend town halls, public hearings, and community meetings to stay connected with the decision-making processes in your area. Your presence and input can influence outcomes and remind leaders that they are accountable to the people they serve.

Conclusion
The landscape of leadership is continuously evolving, shaped by the forces of globalization, technological advancement, environmental challenges, and social change. As these forces redefine the expectations and responsibilities of leaders, the need for ethical, informed, and adaptable leadership has never been greater.

Future leaders will need to navigate an increasingly complex world, balancing national interests with global responsibilities, embracing technological innovation while safeguarding ethical standards, and addressing the urgent challenges of climate change and social justice. At the same time, the role of the citizenry remains crucial in shaping the direction of leadership.
By staying informed, engaging in public discourse, advocating for the issues you care

about, and holding leaders accountable, you play a vital role in ensuring that leadership remains grounded in integrity, transparency, and a commitment to the common good.

In the final chapter, we will reflect on the journey of understanding ethical leadership, the critical role of citizens in fostering such leadership, and how we can all take action to ensure a brighter future for our communities and the world.

Chapter 9: Conclusion – Taking Control of Our Future

Reflecting on Reality: What We've Learned About Leadership

As we reach the end of our exploration into the politics of power, it's essential to reflect on the lessons we've uncovered. Leadership is not just about holding a position of authority; it's about the impact leaders have on those they serve. Throughout this book, we've examined the nature of power, the dangers of greed, the traits of ethical leaders, and the profound consequences that leadership choices can have on communities and societies.

We've learned that power, while often seen as something reserved for the elite, is actually a tool that can be wielded by anyone with influence. Whether at the local, national, or global level, leadership decisions shape the lives of millions. The importance of ethical leadership cannot be overstated—when leaders act with integrity, transparency, and a commitment to the common good, they can uplift entire communities. Conversely, when leaders succumb to greed and self-interest, they can cause widespread harm and suffering.

The Citizen's Responsibility: How We Can All Make a Difference

Leadership is not just the responsibility of those in power; it is a collective effort that involves everyone. As citizens, we have a critical role to play in shaping the quality of leadership we receive. By staying informed, participating in the political process, and holding our leaders accountable, we can help ensure that those who hold power do so with integrity and a focus on the greater good.

Throughout this book, we've discussed practical steps that each of us can take to promote ethical leadership:

- **Researching and Evaluating Leaders:** By thoroughly investigating candidates' backgrounds, policy positions, and communication styles, we can make informed decisions at the ballot box.
- **Engaging in Civic Activities:** Whether it's voting, attending town hall meetings, or joining community organizations, our active participation is essential for fostering a culture of accountability and transparency.
- **Advocating for Ethical Policies:** Supporting causes we believe in, organizing community efforts, and using digital tools to track and hold leaders accountable are all ways we can contribute to positive change.

Preparing for Tomorrow: The Future We Can Build Together

Looking ahead, the challenges we face are significant, but so are the opportunities. The world is rapidly changing, and with these changes come new demands and expectations for leadership. By working together, we can build a future where ethical leadership is not just an aspiration but a reality.

The future we can build together is one where leaders prioritize sustainability, social justice, and global cooperation. It's a future where technology is harnessed for the common good, and where leaders are held to the highest standards of integrity and accountability. By staying engaged, advocating for the issues that matter, and holding our leaders accountable, we can ensure that the future is one of fairness, justice, and prosperity for all.

Final Call to Action: Empowering You to Demand Ethical Leadership

As we conclude this book, I encourage you to take the insights and strategies you've learned and apply them in your own life. Whether it's through voting, advocacy, or community organizing, every action counts in the fight for ethical leadership. The power to shape the future is in your hands, and together, we can make a difference.

Remember that ethical leadership starts with informed and engaged citizens. By demanding integrity, transparency, and accountability from those in power, we can create a world where leaders serve the people with honesty and compassion. Let this be your call to action—empower yourself, empower your community, and together, let's build a better future.

Closing Thoughts: Why Your Role in Leadership Matters

Your role in shaping leadership is crucial. Every decision you make, every vote you cast, every conversation you have about the issues that matter—these are the building blocks of a more just and equitable society. Leadership is not just about those at the top; it's about the collective effort of individuals working together for the common good.

As you move forward, remember that you have the power to influence the direction of your community, your country, and the world. By staying informed, engaged, and committed to ethical principles, you can help ensure that leadership is guided by integrity, transparency, and a commitment to the well-being of all.

Thank you for joining me on this journey. Together, we can create a future where ethical leadership is the norm, not the exception, and where power is used to uplift, not to exploit. Let's take control of our future, one informed decision at a time.

Final Note

As I conclude this journey of writing The Politics of Power: Recognizing Greed and Choosing Ethical Leaders, I am filled with a deep sense of gratitude and reflection. This book represents more than just words on a page—it embodies my passion for promoting ethical leadership and the belief that each of us has the power to make a difference.

Writing this book has been an enlightening experience, one that has deepened my understanding of the complexities of leadership and the importance of integrity in those who hold power. My hope is that this book will serve as a guide and a source of inspiration for you, the reader, as you navigate the ever-changing political landscape and take an active role in shaping the future of your community.

Remember, the power to create change starts with you. Whether you are voting in an election, advocating for justice, or simply having a conversation with a friend, your actions matter. Together, we can build a world where leaders are chosen for their commitment to the common good, where greed is recognized and rejected, and where ethical leadership becomes the norm rather than the exception.

Thank you for joining me on this journey. May the insights and strategies shared in these pages empower you to make informed choices, to demand better from those in power, and to be a beacon of integrity in your own life.

With gratitude and hope,

Rializa Fabiania-Sabido

Appendices

Appendix A: Resources for Further Reading

For those interested in delving deeper into the topics discussed in this book, the following resources offer valuable insights into political ethics, leadership, and civic engagement:

- **Books:**
    - "The Ethics of Leadership" by Joanne B. Ciulla
    - "The Righteous Mind: Why Good People Are Divided by Politics and Religion" by Jonathan Haidt
    - "Leadership and Self-Deception: Getting Out of the Box" by The Arbinger Institute
    - "The Road to Character" by David Brooks
- **Articles:**
    - "The Psychology of Power: How Leadership Affects Behavior" (Harvard Business Review)
    - "Understanding Political Greed: The Case for Ethics in Governance" (Ethics in Public Administration Journal)
    - "Why Transparency Matters: The Impact of Open Leadership on Public Trust" (Journal of Political Ethics)
- **Websites:**
    - Transparency International - An organization dedicated to fighting corruption worldwide.
    - Ethics and Compliance Initiative - Resources on ethical leadership and governance.
    - The Center for Public Integrity - Investigative journalism on ethics and transparency in government.

Appendix B: Community Engagement Checklist

Use this checklist to get started on becoming more involved in your community and promoting ethical leadership:

1. **Stay Informed:**
    - Follow local, state, and national news.
    - Attend city council meetings or watch them online.
    - Subscribe to newsletters from civic organizations.

2. **Participate in Local Government:**
   - Attend town hall meetings and public forums.
   - Volunteer for local campaigns or community boards.
   - Engage in public comment periods for local ordinances and policies.
3. **Build a Network:**
   - Join or form a community group focused on civic engagement.
   - Connect with neighbors and discuss local issues.
   - Partner with local businesses and organizations to support community initiatives.
4. **Advocate for Transparency and Accountability:**
   - Request public records to ensure transparency in local government.
   - Support independent media and investigative journalism.
   - Organize or participate in community watchdog groups.
5. **Vote and Encourage Others to Vote:**
   - Verify your voter registration and find your polling place.
   - Volunteer as a poll worker or help register new voters.
   - Discuss the importance of voting with friends, family, and neighbors.

Appendix C: Sample Questions for Evaluating Leaders

Use these questions to critically assess the ethical qualities of political candidates and leaders:

1. **Integrity and Ethics:**
   - Has the candidate demonstrated consistent ethical behavior in their past roles?
   - Do they have a history of making decisions that prioritize the common good over personal gain?
2. **Transparency:**
   - How open is the candidate about their decision-making processes and financial interests?
   - Do they provide clear, detailed explanations for their policy positions?
3. **Accountability:**
   - How has the candidate responded to criticism or mistakes in the past?
   - Are they willing to admit when they are wrong and take responsibility for their actions?
4. **Empathy and Representation:**
   - Does the candidate listen to and address the concerns of diverse groups within the community?
   - Have they demonstrated a commitment to serving all constituents, not just those with power or influence?

5. **Vision and Long-Term Thinking:**
    - Does the candidate have a clear, positive vision for the future of the community or nation?
    - Are their policies focused on sustainable, long-term solutions rather than short-term gains?

Appendix D: Glossary of Key Terms

- **Accountability:** The obligation of leaders to be answerable for their actions and decisions to the public.
- **Civic Engagement:** The participation of citizens in the political process and community affairs to influence governance and decision-making.
- **Ethical Leadership:** Leadership that is guided by respect for ethical beliefs, values, and the dignity and rights of others.
- **Greed:** Intense and selfish desire for something, especially wealth, power, or material gain, often at the expense of ethical standards.
- **Integrity:** The quality of being honest and having strong moral principles; moral uprightness.
- **Transparency:** The practice of being open, honest, and straightforward about various aspects of governance, including decision-making processes, finances, and policies.
- **Vigilance:** The action or state of keeping careful watch for possible dangers or difficulties, especially in the context of maintaining ethical governance.

Index

A

- **Accountability**
    - Community's role in ensuring
    - Strategies for holding leaders accountable
- **Action, Civic**
    - Importance in leadership
    - Case studies
- **Authority**
    - Nature of power
    - Influence beyond authority

B

- **Bernardo, Rev. Ptr. Joel P.**
    - Acknowledgments
- **Building Movements**
    - Organizing communities for ethical leadership

C

- **Case Studies**
    - Examples of ethical vs. greedy leadership
    - Leadership impacts
    - Community action
- **Community**
    - Role in shaping leadership
    - Accountability measures
- **Corruption**
    - Case studies of
    - Impact on communities
- **Crisis, Leadership**
    - Current global challenges

D

- **Decision-Making**
  - Influence of power on
  - Ethical vs. unethical approaches
- **Democracy**
  - Civic engagement's role in

E

- **Ethical Leadership**
  - Traits of
  - Impact on communities
  - Long-term effects
- **Evaluation of Leaders**
  - Tools for evaluating
  - Researching candidates
- **Examples, Real-World**
  - Greedy leadership
  - Ethical leadership

F

- **Failures in Leadership**
  - Case studies
  - Impact on communities

G

- **Greed**
  - Impact on leadership
  - Case studies of
  - Identifying in leaders

H

- **Honesty in Leadership**
  - Importance of integrity
  - Transparency and trust

I

- **Influence**
  - Nature of power
  - Decision-making
- **Integrity**
  - Defining ethical leadership

J

- **Justice, Social**
  - Role of ethical leaders

L

- **Leadership**
  - Current crisis
  - Power dynamics
  - Impact of
  - Ethical vs. unethical

M

- **Movements, Community**
  - Building for ethical leadership
  - Examples of successful civic engagement

P

- **Power**
  - Nature and definition
  - Influence in communities
  - Consequences of decisions

R

- **Researching Candidates**
  - How to vet political candidates
  - Identifying red flags

- **Responsibility**
  - Citizen's role in leadership

S

- **Sabido, Ruel**
  - Acknowledgments
- **Social Media**
  - Role in modern leadership
  - Misinformation challenges
- **Success in Leadership**
  - Case studies
  - Long-term impact

T

- **Technology**
  - Impact on leadership
  - Role in civic engagement
- **Transparency**
  - Importance in leadership
  - Building trust
- **Trust**
  - Building through transparency
  - Importance in ethical leadership

V

- **Vigilance**
  - Importance of continued citizen involvement
- **Voting**
  - Making your voice count
  - Engaging in the electoral process

W

- **Warnings, Red Flags**
  - Identifying greed in leadership

Y

- **Your Role**
  - Citizen's impact on leadership

About the Author

Rializa Fabiania-Sabido is a dedicated observer of political and social dynamics, with a passion for ethical leadership and community well-being. Though not a politician by trade, Rializa has spent years studying and analyzing the impacts of leadership decisions on real-world communities. Drawing from personal experiences and extensive research, this book provides readers with practical insights into the critical role of leadership in shaping our world. Rializa aims to empower everyday citizens to recognize the signs of greed in leadership and to make informed choices that promote integrity and fairness.

www.ingramcontent.com/pod-product-compliance
Lightning Source LLC
Chambersburg PA
CBHW062125220526
45471CB00010B/3881